How to Pass Digital SAT

The Newest Comprehensive Scholastic Assessment Test Exam Prep Guide with High Score Tips, and Practice Tests for Teens and High School Students

Jordan Sterling

Contents

The Digital SAT in a Nutshell

The SAT, or Scholastic Assessment Test, is a standardized test widely used for college admissions in the United States. The exam is designed to assess a student's readiness for college and provide colleges with a common data point that can be used to compare all applicants. In this chapter, we will explore the structure and format of the digital SAT, with a specific focus on the Reading and Writing and Math sections.

The Digital SAT Format

The digital SAT is composed of two primary sections: the Reading and Writing section and the Math section. These two sections are collectively designed to evaluate a student's skills in critical reading, writing, and mathematical reasoning. Let's take a closer look at each section.

Reading and Writing Section

- **Time Allotted**: Students are given a total of 64 minutes to complete the Reading and Writing section.

- **Number of Modules**: This section is divided into two equal-length modules, each lasting 32 minutes.

- **Total Questions**: In this section, students will encounter a total of 54 questions and tasks.

- **Question Types**: The questions in the Reading and Writing section cover a range of formats, including multiple-choice questions and tasks.

Math Section

- **Time Allotted**: Students have 70 minutes at their disposal to complete the Math section.

- **Number of Modules**: Similar to the Reading and Writing section, the Math section consists of two modules, each lasting 35 minutes.

- **Total Questions**: In the Math section, students will tackle a total of 44 questions.

- **Question Types**: Most of the questions in the Math section are in multiple-choice format. However, some math questions require students to enter the answer directly, rather than selecting it from a list of choices.

Break Time

- **Break**: There is a 10-minute break provided between the Reading and Writing section and the Math section. This gives students a brief opportunity to recharge before tackling the math questions.

Adaptive Nature

- **Question Difficulty**: The SAT is known for its adaptive nature. Based on how you perform on the first module of questions in each section, the second module will be adjusted in terms of difficulty. If a student performs well on the first module, the second module may contain more challenging questions. Conversely, if a student finds the first module more challenging, the second module may consist of less difficult questions.

Guessing

- **No Penalty for Guessing**: It's important to note that there is no penalty for guessing on the SAT. If you are unsure about the answer to a question, it is always better to make an educated guess rather than leaving the response blank.

Time Management

In total, you will have 2 hours and 14 minutes to complete the digital SAT, which includes both sections and the break in between. Effective time management is crucial to ensure that all questions are addressed within the allotted time.

Compared to the ACT, another standardized college admissions test, the SAT provides significantly more time per question. This additional time can be an advantage for students who prefer a more deliberate approach to problem-solving.

Here's a chart for the 2024 Anticipated SAT Test Dates & Registration Deadlines:

Test Date	Est. Registration Deadline	Est. Online Score Release	Format
March 9, 2024	February 23, 2024	March 22-29, 2024	Digital
May 4, 2024	April 19, 2024	May 17-24, 2024	Digital
June 1, 2024	May 16, 2024	June 14-21, 2024	Digital
August 24, 2023	August 8, 2023	September 6-14, 2024	Digital
October 5, 2024	September 20, 2024	October 18-25, 2024	Digital
November 2, 2024	October 18, 2024	November 15-22, 2024	Digital
December 7, 2024	November 22, 2024	December 20-27, 2024	Digital

Please note that the dates and deadlines are estimates and subject to change, so it's important to verify them on the official SAT website closer to your intended test date.

Understanding the SAT

Welcome to your journey towards mastering the SAT! You might be wondering, "What exactly is the SAT, and why is it so important?" The SAT, or Scholastic Assessment Test, is a standardized test widely used for college admissions in the United States. It's designed to assess your readiness for college and provide colleges with a common data point that can be used to compare all applicants.

Colleges use SAT scores, along with your high school GPA, extracurricular activities, letters of recommendation, and personal essays, to make admissions decisions. A high SAT score can enhance your college application and open doors to more educational opportunities. The test measures skills in three core areas: Reading, Writing and Language, and Math.

Changes in the SAT

The SAT has evolved significantly over the years, and one of the most notable changes recently is the shift from a paper-based to a digital format. This change reflects the growing integration of technology in education and aims to make the testing experience more aligned with today's digital learning environment.

Key Differences in the Digital SAT

- **Test Format**: The digital SAT is shorter, lasting two hours instead of three. This change is designed to make the test experience less daunting and more efficient.

- **Sections and Questions**: The new format features two main sections - Reading and Writing, and Math. The Reading and Writing section includes shorter passages with a focus on a variety of topics, while the Math section allows the use of a calculator throughout.

- **Scoring**: Scoring remains on a 1,600-point scale, with no penalty for guessing. This means you should try to answer every question, even if you're unsure of the answer.

- **Tools and Accessibility**: The digital format includes built-in tools like an onscreen calculator and notepad, enhancing the test-taking experience.

- **Convenience and Flexibility**: Taking the SAT digitally means you can use familiar devices, and you'll receive your scores faster.

As you start this journey, remember that understanding the test's format and content is crucial. This book will guide you through each section, provide strategies for success, and offer plenty of practice opportunities to help you feel confident and prepared on test day.

Familiarizing with the Digital SAT Format

Hey there, future SAT conqueror! Ready to dive into the digital world of the SAT? Let's break down what you'll encounter on test day.

1. Reading and Writing Section:

- **What's Inside**: Think of this section as a combo meal. You get a variety of reading passages - some might be from classic literature, some from science articles, and others could be historical documents. Then, there are questions to test how well you understood these passages.

- **Question Types**: You'll answer multiple-choice questions based on these passages. They'll ask you about the main ideas, details, inferences, and sometimes even the author's tone or purpose.

- **Timing**: You get around 60 minutes for this section. It might sound like a marathon, but with practice, you'll be a speed reader in no time!

2. Math Section:

- **Calculator or No Calculator?**: Good news! In the digital SAT, you can use a calculator for the entire Math section. So, make sure your calculator skills are on point.

- **Question Types**: You'll see a mix of multiple-choice and grid-in questions. These will cover Algebra, Advanced Math, Problem Solving, Data Analysis, and even a bit of Geometry and Trigonometry.

- **Timing**: This section gives you 70 minutes. It's all about balancing speed with accuracy. You've got this!

Overall Test Timing:

- The entire test lasts about 2 hours. That's shorter than the old paper-based SAT, giving you more time to focus and less time to stress.

Remember: Each question is a small step towards your goal. Approach them one at a time, and you'll do great!

Next Up: We'll talk about how your hard work is scored and introduce you to the cool digital tools that'll be your allies on test day! Stay tuned, and keep that positive energy flowing!

Scoring Methodology: How the SAT Scores Your Brainpower

In the previous chapter, we delved into the digital SAT's testing format.

The Reading and Writing section, lasting about 60 minutes, offers a variety of passages from literature, science articles, and historical documents, with multiple-choice questions focusing on main ideas, details, inferences, and authorial tone.

The Math section, a 70-minute challenge, allows calculator use throughout and features a mix of multiple-choice and grid-in questions covering Algebra, Advanced Math, Problem Solving, Data Analysis, Geometry, and Trigonometry.

The entire test is streamlined to about 2 hours, shorter than the traditional paper-based SAT, emphasizing efficiency and reduced stress. With each question representing a step towards your goal, a methodical and focused approach is key to success.

Let's move now to the Scoring Methodology.

Understanding the 1,600-Point Scale

Alright, let's talk numbers! Your SAT score is like a gamer's high score, only instead of blasting aliens, you're acing questions. The total score you can achieve on the SAT is 1,600 points. This score comes from two sections: Math and Evidence-Based Reading and Writing. Each section is worth up to 800 points. Add them together, and voilà, you've got your total score!

In the previous chapter, we've learned about the SAT's scoring methodology and its 1,600-point scale. Your total SAT score, which could reach up to 1,600 points, is derived from the sum of the Math and Evidence-Based Reading and Writing sections, each contributing a maximum of 800 points. The raw score, which is the total number of questions you answer correctly in each section, is converted into a scaled score ranging from 200 to 800 per section. This conversion ensures fairness across different test versions. Additionally, your score report includes a percentile rank, showing how your performance compares to other test-takers. What constitutes a "good" SAT score varies depending on the colleges you're applying to, with a score above 1,050 generally considered above average. Importantly, there's no penalty for guessing on the SAT, so it's advantageous to answer every question.

How Do They Add Up the Points?

1. **Each Question Counts**: Each question you answer correctly earns you points. There's no difference in point value between easy and hard questions, so grab those easy points first!

2. **No Fear in Guessing**: Here's some great news – there's no penalty for guessing on the SAT! In the old days, wrong answers used to cost you, but not anymore. If you're stuck, take your best guess. You've got a shot at extra points with no risk of losing any.

3. **The Raw Score**: Your raw score is the total number of questions you answered correctly in a section. So, if you nail 40 questions in the Math section, your raw score for Math is 40.

4. **Conversion to the Scaled Score**: This raw score is then converted into the scaled score – that's the number between 200 and 800 you see on your score report for each section. The College Board uses a fancy process called 'equating' to make sure scores are fair across different test versions.

5. **Composite Score**: Finally, your Math and Evidence-Based Reading and Writing scaled scores are added together. This sum is your total SAT score. So, if you scored 600 in Math and 650 in Evidence-Based Reading and Writing, your total SAT score would be 1,250.

The Percentile Rank

Alongside your score, you'll also see a percentile rank. This tells you how you did compared to other students. For example, if you're in the 75th percentile, you scored better than 75% of the students who took the SAT.

What's a Good Score?

A "good" SAT score depends on where you want to apply. Different colleges have different score expectations. Generally, a score above 1,050 is considered above average, but for more competitive colleges, you might aim higher.

Practice Makes Perfect

Remember, practice can improve your score. Familiarize yourself with the types of questions and the test format. The more comfortable you are with the test, the better you'll likely do.

Next, we'll introduce you to the digital world of the SAT. You'll learn about the digital interface, the Desmos calculator, and other cool features that will be your trusty sidekicks on test day. Stay tuned!

5

Digital Testing Environment: Navigating the New SAT Landscape

In the previous chapter, we've learned about the SAT's scoring methodology and its 1,600-point scale. Your total SAT score, which could reach up to 1,600 points, is derived from the sum of the Math and Evidence-Based Reading and Writing sections, each contributing a maximum of 800 points.

The raw score, which is the total number of questions you answer correctly in each section, is converted into a scaled score ranging from 200 to 800 per section. This conversion ensures fairness across different test versions. Additionally, your score report includes a percentile rank, showing how your performance compares to other test-takers.

What constitutes a "good" SAT score varies depending on the colleges you're applying to, with a score above 1,050 generally considered above average. Importantly, there's no penalty for guessing on the SAT, so it's advantageous to answer every question.

Let's move now to the Digital Testing Environment.

Embracing the Digital Interface

Welcome to the future of testing! The digital SAT brings a whole new experience to the table. Imagine taking the test on a laptop or tablet, in a way that's more aligned with how you learn and interact with technology every day.

1. **The Bluebook App**: This is your digital testing platform. It's user-friendly and designed to make your test-taking experience as smooth as possible. Before the test day, get familiar with Bluebook. It's like doing a walkthrough of a new video game – you want to know where everything is!

2. **Desmos Calculator**: Math wizards and number newbies, rejoice! The digital SAT includes a built-in Desmos calculator. It's a powerful tool for graphing, plotting, and solving those tricky math problems. Spend some time getting to know its features – it's like having a math sidekick!

3. **Online Notepad**: Love jotting down notes or doing quick calculations?

The digital SAT has an online notepad for all your scribbling needs. It's a great space to work out problems or jot down thoughts before selecting your answer.

4. **Navigation Tools**: Moving through the test is a breeze with intuitive navigation tools. You can easily go back and forth between questions, which is super handy if you want to double-check your answers or skip and return to tougher questions.

5. **Countdown Timer**: Keep track of time with the on-screen countdown timer. It's a nifty feature that helps you manage those precious minutes. Don't worry – if the ticking clock makes you nervous, you have the option to hide it.

Practice Makes Perfect

Just like any new game or app, practice makes perfect. Familiarize yourself with these tools before the test. The more comfortable you are with the digital environment, the more you can focus on acing those questions!

Ready to tackle the SAT with these digital superpowers? Up next, we'll go into specific strategies for each section of the test. Let's level up your test-taking skills!

Reading and Writing Section: Unlocking the World of Words

Welcome to the Reading and Writing section of the SAT! This part of the test is like a treasure hunt through the vast world of literature, articles, and historical documents. It's where you get to showcase your reading comprehension skills and your ability to analyze and interpret text.

What's Inside:

Imagine a buffet of reading materials. You might find yourself diving into the imaginative realms of classic literature or navigating the factual terrains of science articles. Sometimes, you'll be time-traveling through historical documents. Each passage is an opportunity to explore new ideas and perspectives.

Question Types:

After each passage, you'll encounter multiple-choice questions. These aren't just any questions; they're keys to unlocking the deeper meaning of the texts. You'll be asked about the main ideas, the finer details, the inferences you can draw, and even the author's tone or purpose. Think of it as detective work, where you're piecing together clues to understand the bigger picture.

Timing:

You have around 60 minutes to journey through this section. It might seem like a lot, but time flies when you're engrossed in interesting reads. With practice, you'll become a speed reader, swiftly navigating through passages and questions with ease and confidence.

So, gear up for an adventure in reading and writing! As you prepare, remember that each passage is a new world to explore, and every question is a step towards understanding that world better. Let's dive in and discover the wonders that await in the Reading and Writing section!

What's Inside the Reading and Writing Section: A Closer Look

In the Reading and Writing section of the SAT, students are presented with an array of reading passages, each offering a unique blend of topics and styles. This section is designed not just to test your ability to read, but also to understand, analyze, and interpret the given texts.

Variety of Reading Passages

1. **Classic Literature**: These passages are selected from well-known works that have stood the test of time. They provide rich narratives, complex characters, and themes that have been discussed across generations. Reading these passages, you'll engage with intricate language and literary devices, offering a chance to demonstrate your ability to comprehend

and appreciate sophisticated writing.

2. **Science Articles**: Here, the focus shifts to more factual and data-driven content. These passages are typically excerpts from scientific journals or publications discussing recent discoveries, experiments, or theories in various fields like biology, physics, or environmental science. The key is to understand the scientific concepts presented and how the authors support their findings with evidence.

3. **Historical Documents**: These can range from foundational governmental texts to speeches and letters by historical figures. Reading these documents requires a different skill set – understanding the historical context, the purpose of the document, and the perspective of the author. It's about connecting the past to the present and interpreting the implications of these texts.

Questions Testing Comprehension

After each passage, you'll encounter a series of multiple-choice questions. These questions are carefully crafted to test different aspects of your reading comprehension:

- **Main Ideas**: What is the central theme or argument of the passage? You'll need to identify the core message that the author is trying to convey.

- **Details**: These questions require a keen eye for specifics. You might be asked to recall certain facts, figures, or even particular phrases used in the passage.

- **Inferences**: Some questions ask you to read between the lines. You'll need to draw conclusions based on the information provided, even if it's not explicitly stated.

- **Author's Tone and Purpose**: Understanding why a passage was written and the author's attitude or perspective is crucial. These questions test your ability to interpret the author's intentions and the effectiveness of their writing style.

Developing Skills for the Section

To excel in this section, it's important to develop a broad range of reading habits, familiarize yourself with different writing styles, and practice identifying key elements in texts. Additionally, practicing with sample questions and passages will help you become more adept at quickly understanding and analyzing a variety of texts.

8

Question Types in the Reading and Writing Section

In the Reading and Writing section of the SAT, the multiple-choice questions are designed to evaluate your comprehension and analytical skills. Each question connects to the passages you've read and varies in what it asks you to identify or interpret. Understanding these question types is key to navigating this section effectively.

Main Idea Questions

- **What They Test**: These questions assess your ability to grasp the overarching theme or primary argument of a passage.

- **Approach**: Look for the most comprehensive statement that summarizes the entire passage. Often, this can be found in the introductory or concluding paragraphs.

Detail-Oriented Questions

- **What They Test**: Your attention to specific information mentioned in the passage, such as facts, figures, names, or dates.

- **Approach**: Pay close attention to the specifics in the passage. It helps to briefly note down key details as you read.

Inference Questions

- **What They Test**: Your ability to draw conclusions from the information provided in the passage, even if it's not directly stated.

- **Approach**: These require a deeper level of understanding. Look at the implied meanings and relationships between ideas in the passage.

Author's Tone and Purpose

- **What They Test**: These questions are about why the author wrote the passage and their attitude or feelings towards the subject matter.

- **Approach**: Pay attention to the language used by the author. Words can often give away the author's feelings and intentions. Look for clues in the style of writing – is it formal, critical, enthusiastic?

Strategy and Structure

- **What They Test**: Understanding how the author has structured their argument or narrative and why certain elements are placed where they are.

- **Approach**: Consider how the passage is organized. What role does each paragraph play in the overall piece? How do the different parts connect to each other?

Practice and Preparation

- **Effective Practice**: Regularly reading a wide range of materials and practicing with past SAT questions can significantly enhance your ability to tackle these questions.

- **Time Management**: Given the time constraints of the section, it's important to practice pacing yourself. Learn to quickly identify the type of question and the most efficient way to find its answer.

- **Answer Selection**: Eliminate clearly wrong answers first. This increases your chances if you need to make an educated guess.

Mastering these question types requires not just reading skill but also strategic thinking. The more you practice, the more intuitive these will become, allowing you to navigate through the Reading and Writing section with greater ease and confidence.

9

Timing in the Reading and Writing Section: Mastering the Clock

The Reading and Writing section of the SAT, allocated around 60 minutes, can initially seem like a race against time. However, with the right approach and practice, you can become adept at managing this segment efficiently.

Understanding the Time Allocation

- **Total Time**: The section is designed to be completed in approximately 60 minutes.

- **Per Passage**: Typically, this section includes several passages. Divide the total time by the number of passages to understand how much time you can spend on each one.

Developing Time Management Skills

- **Practice with a Timer**: Regular practice under timed conditions is essential. Use a timer to simulate test conditions and get a feel for the pace you need to maintain.

- **Reading Strategy**: Develop a reading strategy that balances speed with comprehension. Some students prefer to skim the passage first for a general understanding, then tackle the questions, referring back to the passage for specifics.

- **Answering Questions**: Start with questions you find easier or more straightforward. This approach ensures you secure those points early on and boosts your confidence as you proceed.

Speed Reading Techniques

- **Skimming and Scanning**: Learn to skim for the main idea and scan for specific details. These techniques can significantly reduce the time you spend on each passage.

- **Key Word Spotting**: Train yourself to quickly identify and understand key words and phrases that are crucial to answering the questions.

Dealing with Challenging Passages

- **Don't Get Stuck**: If you find a passage particularly challenging, don't spend too much time on it. Move on to other questions and return to it if time permits.

- **Educated Guessing**: Remember, there's no penalty for wrong answers. If you're running out of time, it's better to make an educated guess than to leave questions unanswered.

Final Tips

- **Regular Practice**: The more you practice, the more familiar you will become with the types of passages and questions, which can help improve your speed and efficiency.

- **Stay Calm**: Keeping a calm and focused mind is crucial for efficient time management. Stress and anxiety can slow you down, so practice relaxation techniques if necessary.

Becoming a speed reader in this section is less about rushing through the material and more about developing a strategic approach to reading and answering questions. With consistent practice and a focus on time management, you'll find that 60 minutes is enough to showcase your reading and writing prowess effectively.

10

A Summary of the Reading and Writing Section

Over the last three chapters, we've explored the Reading and Writing section of the SAT, offering insights and strategies to help you excel.

In the chapter about "What's Inside," we saw that this section is a diverse mix of reading materials, from classic literature and science articles to historical documents. This variety not only tests your comprehension skills but also enriches your understanding and appreciation of different writing styles and subjects.

Moving to the "Question Types" chapter, we focused on the multiple-choice questions following each passage. These questions cover main ideas, specific details, inferences, and the author's tone and purpose. We learned that tackling these questions requires a blend of careful reading, critical thinking, and analytical skills. The key is to understand not just what is being said, but how and why it's being said.

In the chapter on "Timing," we addressed the challenge of the 60-minute time limit for this section. Effective time management is crucial, and with practice, you can develop a strategy that allows you to read efficiently and answer questions accurately within the allotted time. Techniques like skimming, scanning, and keyword spotting are invaluable, as is the ability to remain calm and focused under time pressure.

Each of these chapters builds towards a comprehensive approach to mastering the Reading and Writing section. Remember, practice is essential. The more you engage with different types of texts and question styles, the more confident and proficient you'll become. So, keep practicing, stay positive, and believe in your ability to achieve great results!

Introduction to the Math Section: A Journey Through Numbers and Logic

In the Math Section of the SAT, we're about to journey through a landscape rich with numbers, shapes, and logical reasoning.

This section serves as a platform for you to showcase your mathematical skills, a space where you navigate the intricacies of algebraic expressions, geometric shapes, complex data sets, and more.

As we move forward, we will explore in detail the fundamental concepts critical to the SAT. You will encounter the intricate world of Algebra, where variables and equations form the basis of complex problem-solving. In Advanced Math, the challenges increase, presenting scenarios that require a deeper level of mathematical reasoning.

The journey then takes you through the realm of Problem Solving and Data Analysis, where numbers tell stories, and data reveals truths. Here, your skills in interpreting and analyzing information will be paramount. Geometry and Trigonometry offer a different flavor, where the physical space and shapes around us translate into mathematical questions.

Beyond these concepts, the focus will shift to practice problems. These problems are not just questions but opportunities to apply what you've learned, to test your understanding, and to prepare for the actual test environment. Accompanying each problem will be solutions and explanations – tools for learning and understanding, ensuring that you grasp the logic behind each answer.

The digital SAT brings with it the convenience of an onscreen calculator, and we will guide you on how to make the most of this tool. It's about knowing when to rely on it and when to trust your mental math skills.

Finally, we will hone in on strategies specifically tailored for the Math section. Time management is an art, and you will learn how to allocate your minutes wisely. Problem-solving techniques will be discussed in detail, helping you approach each question with a clear strategy. We will also shine a light on common pitfalls, helping you steer clear of them.

In summary, our upcoming chapters are designed to prepare you thoroughly for the Math section of the SAT. It's a journey through various mathematical terrains, each offering its unique challenges and learning opportunities. The aim is not just to teach you math but to equip you with the skills and strategies needed for success in this crucial part of the SAT.

12

Math Fundamentals: Building the Foundation for SAT Success

In the Math Fundamentals chapter, our focus is on building a strong foundation in key mathematical areas essential for the SAT. This section of the SAT isn't just about solving problems; it's about understanding the underlying principles that govern these problems. Let's explore each area in detail.

Algebra: The Language of Equations

- **Understanding Equations and Inequalities**: At the heart of algebra lies the ability to work with equations and inequalities. You'll learn how to solve for unknown variables, whether they are tucked away in linear equations or hidden in more complex quadratic forms.

- **Systems of Equations**: Often, you will encounter problems where multiple equations interact. Mastering systems of equations means learning to find common solutions that satisfy all equations in the system.

Advanced Math: Beyond the Basics

- **Functions and Their Applications**: Functions are fundamental in understanding how different variables relate to each other. You'll explore different types of functions, including linear, quadratic, and exponential, and learn how to interpret their graphs.

- **Complex Equations**: Here, you'll encounter equations that require a more advanced approach. This includes understanding higher-degree polynomials and tackling equations with multiple variables.

Problem Solving and Data Analysis: Numbers in Context

- **Real-World Data Interpretation**: This section is all about applying math to real life. You'll learn to interpret data sets, understand probability and statistics, and solve problems involving ratios, percentages, and proportional reasoning.

- **Critical Analysis of Data**: We'll also focus on how to critically analyze the data presented to you. This means not just understanding the numbers but also questioning and interpreting the data in a meaningful way.

Geometry and Trigonometry: Shapes, Spaces, and Measures

- **Geometry**: Geometry questions on the SAT cover a wide range of concepts, from the properties of angles and triangles to the characteristics of circles and polygons. You'll explore how to calculate areas, perimeters, and volumes, as well as understanding theorems and postulates that are pivotal to solving geometric problems.

- **Trigonometry**: Trigonometry in the SAT isn't just about sine, cosine, and tangent; it's about applying these concepts to solve problems. This includes understanding the relationships in right-angled triangles and the properties of trigonometric functions.

Each of these areas will be broken down to its core concepts, with an emphasis on understanding rather than just memorizing formulas. The goal is to equip you with a deep understanding of these mathematical principles, so you can approach SAT questions with confidence and clarity. As we progress, remember that each concept builds upon the last, forming a comprehensive picture of the mathematical knowledge needed for the SAT.

13

Practice Problems: Honing Your Mathematical Skills

In this chapter, we turn our focus to practice problems, an essential part of your SAT preparation. These problems are not just exercises; they are a window into the types of questions you will encounter on the actual SAT. They are meticulously designed to reflect the style and complexity of the SAT, ensuring that you are well-prepared for the range of questions you might face.

The Essence of Practice Problems

- **Diverse Question Types**: The practice problems encompass a wide range of mathematical topics covered in the SAT. You'll find questions on algebra, advanced math, data analysis, geometry, and trigonometry, each tailored to test different aspects of your mathematical understanding.

- **Real SAT Experience**: The format and presentation of these questions mirror the actual SAT. This design gives you a realistic taste of the SAT environment, helping you to become familiar with the way questions are posed and the kind of reasoning they require.

Solutions and Explanations

- **Detailed Solutions**: Every practice problem is accompanied by a comprehensive solution. These solutions don't just give you the answer; they walk you through the process of solving the problem, step by step.

- **Understanding the 'Why'**: The explanations focus on the rationale behind each solution. This approach helps you understand the underlying principles and methods needed to solve similar problems.

- **Learning from Mistakes**: Where common mistakes are likely, the explanations highlight these pitfalls. This insight is invaluable in helping you avoid similar errors in the actual test.

Approach to Practice

- **Systematic Practice**: It's recommended to approach these problems systematically. Start with areas you find challenging to strengthen your weak spots.

- **Regular Review**: Regularly revisit problems, especially those you initially found difficult. This repetition ensures the concepts and methods become second nature.

- **Time Yourself**: Practice under timed conditions to get used to the pace required for the SAT. As you become more proficient, your speed and accuracy should improve.

Practice is the cornerstone of success in the Math section of the SAT. By working through these problems, reviewing the solutions, and understanding the explanations, you will build a strong foundation in mathematical concepts and problem-solving techniques. This preparation will not only aid you in achieving a high score on the SAT but will also enhance your overall mathematical proficiency.

14

Calculator Tips: Mastering the Digital Tool

In the Math section of the SAT, the digital format introduces an onscreen calculator, transforming it into a valuable ally for tackling a variety of mathematical problems. This chapter is dedicated to helping you harness the full potential of this tool, ensuring it enhances your problem-solving process.

Understanding When to Use the Calculator

- **Efficiency is Key**: The calculator is a powerful tool, but it's not always necessary. Recognize situations where using the calculator will save time and where it might actually slow you down. For basic arithmetic or simple algebraic equations, you might find that solving them mentally or on paper is quicker.

- **Complex Calculations**: Use the calculator for more complex calculations, like those involving decimals, higher-order equations, or trigono-metric functions. This minimizes errors and saves time.

Navigating the Calculator Effectively

- **Familiarize with Functions**: Before the test, spend time getting to know the functions and layout of the onscreen calculator. Knowing where to find specific functions (like square roots, exponents, or trigonometric functions) can save valuable time during the test.

- **Practice Makes Perfect**: Incorporate the calculator into your practice sessions. This not only helps with familiarity but also allows you to gauge when its use is most beneficial.

Calculator Tips and Tricks

- **Shortcut Techniques**: Learn any shortcut techniques that the calculator offers. For instance, using memory functions to store and recall values can be a real time-saver.

- **Checking Your Work**: The calculator can be an excellent tool for checking your work. After solving a problem manually, use the calculator to verify your answer.

- **Avoid Over-reliance**: While the calculator is helpful, over-reliance can be a pitfall. Ensure you understand the underlying mathematical concepts and don't just depend on the calculator to do all the work.

Dealing with Potential Issues

- **Technical Glitches**: Be prepared for the possibility of technical issues. Knowing how to quickly reset or troubleshoot basic problems with the calculator can prevent panic during the test.

- **Battery Life**: Although this is less of a concern with an onscreen calculator, always ensure your device is fully charged if you're using a personal device for the test.

In summary, the onscreen calculator is a significant asset in the digital SAT Math section. By understanding when and how to use it efficiently, you can make this tool work to your advantage. Remember, the calculator should aid your problem-solving, not become a crutch. A balanced approach, combining mental math skills and calculator efficiency, will set you on the path to success.

Math Test Strategies: Navigating the SAT with Skill and Precision

In the Math section of the SAT, how you approach the problems is just as important as your ability to solve them. This chapter is dedicated to equipping you with effective strategies for time management, problem-solving, and avoiding common pitfalls.

Time Management: Mastering the Clock

- **Understand the Time Allocation**: You have a limited amount of time to answer all the questions in the Math section. It's crucial to understand how to divide this time across different types of problems.

- **Prioritize Questions**: Not all questions are created equal. Begin with problems that seem more straightforward or familiar to you. This strategy ensures you secure easy points early on and boosts your confidence.

- **Set Time Limits**: Practice setting time limits for each question during your preparation. This helps develop a sense of how long to spend on a problem before moving on.

Problem-Solving Techniques

- **Read Carefully**: Misreading a question can lead to incorrect answers. Take a moment to thoroughly read and understand what each question is asking.

- **Break Down the Problem**: Complex problems can often be made simpler by breaking them down into smaller, more manageable parts.

- **Work Backwards**: For some questions, especially those involving multiple-choice answers, it can be effective to work backwards. Start with the given answers and see which one fits best.

- **Draw Diagrams**: Visual aids like graphs, charts, and diagrams can be incredibly helpful, especially in geometry questions.

- **Estimate and Approximate**: Sometimes, an exact answer isn't necessary. Estimation can be a useful tool for narrowing down answer choices.

Avoiding Common Pitfalls

- **Overcomplicating Solutions**: The simplest solution is often the right one. Be wary of overcomplicating your approach to a problem.

- **Misusing the Calculator**: While the calculator is a useful tool, inappropriate use can lead to errors. Be sure to double-check your calculator inputs and outputs.

- **Ignoring Units**: Pay attention to units of measurement. Incorrect units can lead to incorrect answers.

- **Rushing Through Problems**: While time is of the essence, rushing can lead to careless errors. It's important to find a balance between speed and accuracy.

Practice Makes Perfect

- **Simulate Test Conditions**: Regularly practice under conditions that mimic the actual SAT. This includes timing yourself and using the same type of calculator you'll use on test day.

- **Review Mistakes**: Take the time to review and understand each mistake you make during practice. This not only helps you correct misunderstandings but also prevents similar errors in the actual test.

Mastering these strategies will require practice and dedication. Remember, the goal is not just to solve math problems but to do so in a way that is both efficient and effective. By internalizing these techniques and approaches, you'll be well-equipped to tackle the Math section of the SAT with confidence and precision. Stay persistent in your preparation, and you'll see your skills and speed improve over time.

16

Summarizing Your Journey Through the Math Section

In our exploration of the Math section for the SAT, we've covered a comprehensive range of topics and strategies, all aimed at bolstering your mathematical prowess and test-taking confidence.

Math Fundamentals: We started by building a solid foundation in key math areas. From the language of equations in Algebra to the complex scenarios in Advanced Math, and from the practical applications in Problem Solving and Data Analysis to the geometric and trigonometric challenges in Geometry and Trigonometry, each topic was unpacked to ensure a thorough understanding. This approach is designed to not just prepare you for the SAT but also to enhance your overall appreciation for mathematics.

Practice Problems: Next, we dived into practice problems, which are the crucible where your mathematical skills are tested and refined. These problems are a mirror to the actual SAT, crafted to reflect the exam's style and complexity. Accompanying each problem were detailed solutions and explanations, turning every challenge into a learning opportunity and ensuring that you understand the 'why' behind each answer.

Calculator Tips: The chapter on calculator tips was all about mastering this digital tool, which can be a game-changer in the Math section. We discussed when to use the calculator to your advantage and when it might be quicker to rely on mental math. The focus was on using the calculator efficiently, ensuring it aids your problem-solving process without becoming a crutch.

Math Test Strategies: Finally, we tackled strategies specific to the Math section. Time management emerged as a key theme, emphasizing the importance of balancing speed with accuracy. We explored various problem-solving techniques, from breaking down complex problems to working backwards from the answers. Recognizing and avoiding common pitfalls was another crucial topic, helping you navigate through the section without stumbling over frequent errors.

As you prepare for the Math section of the SAT, remember that each concept you learn and each problem you solve is a step towards not just a great score, but also a deeper understanding of mathematics. Keep practicing, stay curious, and approach each challenge with a problem-solver's mindset. You're not just preparing for a test; you're gearing up for a world where math is a valuable tool. So, embrace the journey, and let your hard work and dedication lead you to success!

17

Test-Taking Strategies - Navigating the SAT with Confidence

In the previous chapters, we walked through two parts of the SAT exam, the Reading and Writing part, and the Math part. Now, let's talk about the strategies that can help you excel in these areas.

This section is specifically designed to provide you with the tools and insights needed to approach the test with a strategic mindset. It's about more than just understanding the material; it's about mastering the approach to the test, managing your time effectively, making smart choices under pressure, and maintaining your focus and calm throughout the exam. These skills are essential in maximizing your performance and achieving your best possible score on the SAT.

Chapters Overview

1. **Time Management**: In the next chapter, we will explore various techniques for managing your time during the test. Time management is crucial in a timed exam like the SAT. You'll learn how to allocate your time across different sections and question types, ensuring that you have the opportunity to answer every question to the best of your ability. We'll cover how to quickly assess questions, determine the amount of time to spend on each, and how to keep track of time without letting it become a source of stress.

2. **Guessing and Question Navigation**: The following chapter focuses on strategies for making educated guesses and effectively navigating through questions. Sometimes, an educated guess can be your best friend on a test like the SAT. We'll discuss how to identify when it's appropriate to guess and techniques for increasing the likelihood of a correct guess. Additionally, you'll learn how to use the SAT's 'mark-for-review' and 'strikethrough' tools to your advantage, helping you organize your thoughts and manage your time more effectively.

3. **Dealing with Test Anxiety**: The final chapter for test-aking strate-

gies is all about handling test anxiety. It's normal to feel some level of nervousness before and during the test, but it's important to keep this anxiety in check. We'll share tips for staying calm and focused, from breathing exercises to positive visualization techniques. You'll learn how to prepare mentally and emotionally for the test, ensuring that anxiety doesn't stand in the way of your performance.

18

Time Management: Mastering the Clock in the SAT

Effective time management is a critical skill for success on the SAT. This comprehensive chapter is designed to help you develop strategies to utilize every minute of the exam efficiently, ensuring that you can give your best performance across all sections.

Understanding the SAT Time Allocation

The SAT is a timed test, and each section has a specific time limit. It's crucial to know these limits and plan accordingly. For instance, the Reading section might allow you a total of 65 minutes for 52 questions, while the Math section gives you 80 minutes for 58 questions. Familiarize yourself with the time allocated for each section and the average time you should spend per question.

Developing a Time Management Plan

- **Create a Plan**: Before the test, have a clear plan for how you will allocate your time. For example, you might decide to spend no more than a minute per question on the easier problems, allowing more time for the challenging ones.

- **Practice with Timers**: During your preparation, use timers to simulate the test environment. This helps you get a real feel for the pace you need to maintain.

- **Adapt Your Reading Speed**: For the Reading section, learn to adjust your reading speed. Skim passages for easier questions and slow down for complex ones requiring deeper analysis.

Quick Assessment of Questions

- **Identify Question Types**: Quickly assess each question and categorize it – is it easy, medium, or hard for you? Tackle the easy ones first to secure quick points.

- **Prioritize Questions**: Not all questions are worth the same amount of time. Learn to recognize which questions you can answer quickly and which ones might need more time.

Balancing Speed and Accuracy

- **Avoid Rushing**: While it's important to be aware of time, rushing through questions can lead to careless mistakes. Strike a balance between speed and accuracy.

- **Review Your Answers**: If time permits, go back and review your answers, especially in sections where you had to guess or were unsure.

Keeping Track of Time During the Exam

- **Use the Clock Wisely**: Keep an eye on the clock, but don't let it dominate your focus. Regular checks can help ensure you're on track without causing stress.

- **Setting Mini-Goals**: Break the section down into smaller chunks and set mini-goals. For instance, aim to complete a certain number of questions in 20 minutes.

Dealing with Time Pressure

- **Stay Calm**: If you find yourself running out of time, stay calm. Panicking can slow you down. Focus on answering the questions you know first.

- **Educated Guessing**: Learn when to move on and make an educated guess. This skill is crucial for questions that are taking too long.

Adjusting Your Strategy

- **Be Flexible**: Be prepared to adjust your strategy if things don't go as planned. Flexibility is key in adapting to the flow of the exam.

- **Reflect on Practice Tests**: After taking practice tests, reflect on your time management. Were there sections where you consistently ran out of time? Adjust your strategy accordingly.

Time management on the SAT is about finding the right balance between speed and careful consideration of each question. It involves a combination of planning, practice, and adaptability. By mastering these strategies, you can ensure that time is on your side during the SAT, enabling you to showcase your true capabilities. Remember, practice is essential - the more you familiarize yourself with these techniques, the more instinctive they will become on test day. Stay focused, stay calm, and let your preparation guide you to success.

19

Guessing and Question Navigation: Smart Strategies for the SAT

In this chapter, we focus on mastering the art of making educated guesses and effectively navigating through SAT questions. In a high-stakes test like the SAT, where every point counts, knowing when and how to guess can be a strategic advantage.

Understanding Educated Guessing

- **No Penalty for Wrong Answers**: Remember, the SAT does not penalize for wrong answers. This means an educated guess is always better than leaving a question blank.

- **Identifying Guessable Questions**: Learn to recognize the questions where you can make a logical guess. This often involves eliminating one or more obviously incorrect answer choices to improve your odds of guessing correctly.

Techniques for Making Educated Guesses

- **Process of Elimination**: Use the process of elimination to narrow down your choices. Even if you can eliminate one or two options, your chances of guessing the right answer increase significantly.

- **Looking for Clues**: Sometimes, the test itself can give you hints. Look for clues in the question and other answer choices that might point you toward the correct answer or away from wrong ones.

Navigating Questions Effectively

- **Utilizing 'Mark-for-Review'**: The SAT allows you to mark questions for review. Use this feature to flag questions you are unsure about so you can return to them later if time permits.

- **Strategic Question Order**: Tackle the questions in the order that suits you best. Some students prefer to answer all the questions they find easy first, then go back to the harder ones.

The 'Strikethrough' Tool

- **Eliminating Distractions**: The 'strikethrough' feature lets you cross out options you believe are incorrect. This can help clear your mind and focus on the remaining choices.

- **Visual Clarity**: Striking through wrong answers provides a visual aid in focusing on potentially correct choices, making it easier to compare them and make a final decision.

Managing Your Time

- **Balancing Speed and Accuracy**: While guessing can save time, it's important to balance this with the effort to solve as many problems as accurately as possible. Don't rush to guess – use it as a strategic tool when needed.

- **Timing for Review**: Allocate the last few minutes of each section to revisit the questions you marked for review. This is where you can take your final guesses or change answers if you have new insights.

Making educated guesses and navigating questions effectively are skills that can significantly impact your SAT performance. These strategies are about playing the odds in your favor and using the test format to your advantage. With practice, you can become adept at knowing when to guess, how to eliminate choices, and how to use the tools provided to organize your approach. Remember, the goal is to maximize your score, and sometimes, a smart guess is an essential part of that strategy. Stay focused, stay strategic, and use every tool at your disposal to conquer the SAT.

20

Dealing with Test Anxiety: Staying Calm and Focused

As we approach this chapter, it's important to address a common challenge many students face: test anxiety. It's completely normal to feel a certain level of nervousness before and during the SAT. You are not alone in this. Many students experience this kind of stress, but the key lies in managing it effectively so that it doesn't hinder your performance.

Understanding Test Anxiety

- **Recognizing the Symptoms**: Test anxiety can manifest in various ways – from butterflies in your stomach to more severe symptoms like headaches or nausea. Recognizing these signs is the first step in managing them.

- **It's a Natural Reaction**: Remember, a certain level of stress is a natural reaction to challenging situations. It can even be beneficial, keeping you alert and focused.

Techniques to Manage Anxiety

- **Breathing Exercises**: Deep, controlled breathing can be a powerful tool to calm your nerves. Practice breathing exercises where you inhale slowly, hold your breath for a few seconds, and then exhale slowly. This helps lower your heart rate and relax your mind.

- **Positive Visualization**: Imagine yourself succeeding in the test. Visualization techniques can create a positive mindset and reduce anxiety.

- **Preparation is Key**: Being well-prepared can significantly reduce anxiety. The more familiar you are with the material and the test format, the more confident you'll feel.

On the Day of the Test

- **Healthy Routine**: Start your test day with a good breakfast and some light exercise. This can help in reducing stress levels.

- **Arrive Early**: Get to the test center early to avoid any last-minute rushes, which can increase anxiety.

- **Comfortable Environment**: Make sure you're dressed comfortably and have everything you need for the test.

During the Test

- **Stay Hydrated**: Keep a bottle of water handy. Staying hydrated helps in maintaining focus and keeping calm.

- **Take Short Breaks**: During the test, if you feel overwhelmed, take a short mental break. Close your eyes for a moment, take a few deep breaths, and then refocus on the test.

- **Focus on the Present**: Try to focus on the question at hand and not on the outcome of the test. This helps in maintaining concentration and reduces stress.

Post-Test Strategies

- **Reflect Positively**: Regardless of how you think you did, reflect on the effort you put in rather than the outcome.

- **Relax and Reward Yourself**: After the test, do something you enjoy. This helps in releasing any residual stress.

Remember, feeling anxious about a significant test like the SAT is natural. However, with the right strategies and a positive mindset, you can manage this anxiety effectively. Your mental and emotional preparation is as important as your academic preparation. Embrace these techniques, and you'll be well on your way to not just facing the SAT but conquering it with confidence and calm.

21

Summarizing Strategies for SAT Success

In the recent chapters of our SAT preparation guide, we've been learning strategies that can help you navigate the SAT with confidence and skill. These strategies are not just about mastering the material but also about effectively approaching the test itself.

In the **Time Management** chapter, we explored various techniques to manage your time during the exam. You learned how to allocate time across different sections and question types, ensuring the opportunity to answer every question well. The focus was on assessing questions quickly, determining the right amount of time to spend on each, and keeping track of time without becoming overwhelmed.

The **Guessing and Question Navigation** chapter provided strategies for making educated guesses and effectively navigating through questions. We discussed when it's appropriate to guess and techniques to increase the likelihood of a correct guess. You also learned how to use the SAT's 'mark-for-review' and 'strikethrough' tools, which can be instrumental in organizing your thoughts and managing your time more effectively during the test.

Finally, the **Dealing with Test Anxiety** chapter addressed the common issue of nervousness before and during the test. We shared tips for staying calm and focused, including breathing exercises and positive visualization techniques. This chapter aimed to help you prepare mentally and emotionally for the test, ensuring that anxiety doesn't impede your performance.

Together, these chapters provided a comprehensive approach to mastering the SAT. They equipped you with practical skills and strategies to approach the test efficiently, making the most of your knowledge and preparation. Remember, with the right approach and mindset, you can tackle the SAT confidently and successfully.

22

Introduction to Full-Length Practice Tests - Your Path to Mastery

As we move into the practical part of our SAT preparation guide, we transition from learning and strategy development to application and practice. This part is dedicated to Full-Length Practice Tests, a crucial component of your SAT preparation.

The Role of Full-Length Practice Tests

Full-length digital SAT practice tests are invaluable tools in your SAT prep arsenal. They serve several key purposes:

1. **Real-World Simulation**: These tests simulate the actual test environment, giving you a realistic experience of what to expect on the day of the exam. This includes the format, the types of questions, and the time

constraints.

2. **Application of Knowledge and Strategies**: After learning the content and strategies in the previous chapters, these practice tests allow you to apply what you've learned in a setting that mimics the real SAT.

3. **Identifying Strengths and Weaknesses**: By taking these tests, you'll be able to identify areas where you excel and areas that need more focus. This insight is crucial for targeted studying in the final stages of your preparation.

Structure of the Practice Tests

- **Comprehensive Coverage**: Each practice test covers all sections of the SAT, ensuring a thorough review of all topics.

- **Timed Format**: The tests adhere to the same time constraints as the actual SAT, helping you practice time management under exam conditions.

Detailed Answer Explanations

One of the most valuable aspects of these practice tests is the detailed answer explanations provided for each question. These explanations offer:

- **Understanding of Correct Answers**: Not only do you learn the correct answer, but you also understand the reasoning and methodology behind it.

- **Learning from Mistakes**: For questions you get wrong, the explanations help you understand where you went wrong and how to avoid similar mistakes in the future.

- **Reinforcement of Concepts**: Often, these explanations reinforce concepts and strategies covered in earlier chapters, solidifying your understanding and recall.

How to Use the Practice Tests Effectively

- **Regular Practice**: Incorporate these full-length tests into your regular study schedule. Consistent practice is key to improvement.

- **Review and Reflect**: After each test, spend time reviewing your answers, especially the ones you got wrong. Reflect on why you made errors and how you can improve.

- **Simulate Test Conditions**: Try to take these practice tests under conditions that closely mimic the actual test day – this includes adhering to the time limits and taking the test in a quiet, uninterrupted environment.

- **Track Your Progress**: Keep track of your scores on these practice tests to monitor your progress. This can be a great motivator and guide in your study journey.

23

Reading Test: 65 MINUTES, 52 QUESTIONS

Welcome to this section of the practice material, which is designed to prepare you for the Reading component of the SAT exam. In this section, you will find a series of five distinct reading passages. Each passage is followed by a set of questions, totaling 10 for each passage, crafted to test your reading comprehension and analytical skills from various angles.

The passages span a range of topics and styles, from scientific discussions and historical narratives to cultural analyses and explorations of social phenomena. This diversity in content mirrors the actual SAT test, providing you with a comprehensive practice experience.

After each passage, you will encounter questions that are designed to evaluate different aspects of your comprehension and critical thinking. These questions include, but are not limited to:

- **Main Idea**: Identifying the central theme or primary focus of the passage.

- **Detail-Oriented Questions**: Focusing on specific facts or pieces of information presented in the text.

- **Inference**: Drawing logical conclusions based on the information provided in the passage.

- **Character Analysis**: Understanding and interpreting the actions, motivations, or perspectives of individuals in the passage.

- **Textual Evidence**: Citing specific parts of the text to support your answers or interpretations.

- **Comparing and Contrasting**: Examining similarities and differences in concepts, themes, or viewpoints within the passage.

- **Word Meaning in Context**: Deciphering the meaning of specific words or phrases as they are used in the context of the passage.

- **Author's Purpose and Perspective**: Understanding the author's intention behind writing the passage and their viewpoint on the subject matter.

These questions are structured to cover all approaches to test your comprehension and interpretation of the text from different angles. They are designed not only to assess your ability to understand and process written information but also to evaluate your critical thinking and analytical skills.

As you work through these passages and questions, remember that this practice is an opportunity to enhance your reading skills, expand your understanding, and prepare for the types of challenges you will encounter in the actual SAT exam. Good luck!

DIRECTIONS:

Prepare paper, a pen, and a calculator. Remember, you will be taking a digital exam; now you are only practicing.

Each passage or pair of passages below is followed by a number of questions.

After reading each passage or pair, choose the best answer to each question based on what is stated or implied in the passage.

SET A CLOCK TO 65 MINUTES, AND START

Reading Passage 1: "The Impact of Renewable Energy"

In the past two decades, renewable energy has emerged as a key player in the global effort to reduce carbon emissions and combat climate change. Unlike traditional fossil fuels, sources like wind, solar, and hydroelectric power offer a sustainable alternative that minimizes environmental impact. The shift towards renewable energy is not only a technological challenge but also a socio-economic one. It requires significant investment in new infrastructure and a rethinking of energy consumption patterns worldwide. This movement has sparked a global conversation about the balance between economic growth and environmental preservation.

Questions:

1. **Main Idea**: What is the primary focus of the passage?

  - a) The technological advancements in renewable energy.

    ◦ b) The economic impact of shifting to renewable energy.

    ◦ c) The global effort to reduce carbon emissions through renewable energy.

    ◦ d) The challenges in the implementation of renewable energy.

2. **Inference**: What can be inferred about the author's viewpoint on renewable energy?

    ◦ a) The author is skeptical about its feasibility.

    ◦ b) The author views it as a necessary step for environmental preservation.

    ◦ c) The author believes it has limited impact on carbon emissions.

    ◦ d) The author focuses mainly on the economic drawbacks.

3. **Detail-Oriented**: According to the passage, which of the following is NOT mentioned as a source of renewable energy?

    ◦ a) Wind

○ b) Solar

○ c) Nuclear

○ d) Hydroelectric

4. **Author's Purpose**: Why does the author mention "socio-economic" challenges in the passage?

○ a) To highlight the need for global policy changes.

○ b) To emphasize the cost of renewable energy.

○ c) To illustrate the multifaceted nature of transitioning to renewable energy.

○ d) To argue against the reliance on traditional fossil fuels.

5. **Contextual Understanding**: The passage suggests that transitioning to renewable energy involves:

○ a) Only technological development.

○ b) An increase in global carbon emissions.

○ c) Changes in both infrastructure and energy consumption habits.

○ d) Immediate economic benefits for all countries.

6. **Analyzing Arguments**: The passage implies that the shift to renewable energy:

   ○ a) Is primarily a technological challenge.

   ○ b) Faces resistance due to its high costs.

   ○ c) Is crucial for both environmental and economic reasons.

   ○ d) Has been widely accepted without much debate.

7. **Evaluating Evidence**: Which statement from the passage best supports the need for a "rethinking of energy consumption patterns"?

   ○ a) "Renewable energy...minimizes environmental impact."

   ○ b) "The shift towards renewable energy is...a socio-economic one."

   ○ c) "Significant investment in new infrastructure is required."

   ○ d) "This movement has sparked a global conversation..."

8. **Comparing and Contrasting**: How does renewable energy differ from traditional fossil fuels, as mentioned in the passage?

- a) It is less efficient in energy production.

- b) It offers a sustainable alternative with less environmental impact.

- c) It is more expensive and less accessible.

- d) It has been the primary source of energy for decades.

Reading Passage 2: "The Evolution of Communication Technology"

Over the centuries, communication technology has evolved dramatically. From the days of carrier pigeons and telegraphs to the era of the internet and smartphones, each advancement has significantly impacted how we interact and share information. This evolution has not only made communication faster and more efficient but also brought about significant cultural and societal changes. The internet, in particular, has transformed the global landscape, creating a virtual space where ideas, news, and opinions can be shared across the world in real-time. However, this rapid development also poses challenges, such as information overload and concerns about privacy and misinformation.

Questions:

1. **Main Idea**: What is the central focus of the passage?

  - a) The historical development of communication methods.

  - b) The cultural impact of the internet.

  - c) Challenges posed by modern communication technologies.

  - d) The role of smartphones in global communication.

2. **Detail-Oriented**: According to the passage, which of the following was used as an early form of communication?

  - a) Radio signals

  - b) Carrier pigeons

  - c) Emails

  - d) Online forums

3. **Inference**: What can be inferred about the impact of the internet on

communication?

- a) It has made communication less personal.

- b) It has slowed down the pace of information exchange.

- c) It has globalized communication, making it instantaneous and widespread.

- d) It has decreased the reliability of information.

4. **Author's Purpose**: Why does the author mention "information overload" and "concerns about privacy and misinformation"?

- a) To argue against the use of modern communication technologies.

- b) To highlight the negative aspects of communication evolution.

- c) To present challenges associated with the advancement of communication technology.

- d) To suggest a return to traditional communication methods.

5. **Comparing and Contrasting**: How does the passage contrast modern

communication technologies with earlier methods?

- a) By emphasizing the slower pace of historical methods.

- b) By highlighting the limited reach of earlier technologies.

- c) By focusing on the personal nature of traditional communication.

- d) By discussing the technological complexity of earlier methods.

6. **Evaluating Consequences**: What potential consequence of modern communication technology is suggested in the passage?

- a) A decline in traditional cultural practices.

- b) An increase in global connectivity and information sharing.

- c) A rise in privacy violations and the spread of misinformation.

- d) The complete replacement of face-to-face interactions.

7. **Contextual Understanding**: The passage suggests that the evolution of communication technology has:

- a) Led to a more isolated and disconnected society.

- b) Made communication more cumbersome and complex.

- c) Enabled faster and more efficient ways of sharing information.

- d) Reduced the overall amount of communication globally.

8. **Analyzing Effects**: According to the passage, one significant cultural change resulting from communication technology is:

- a) The creation of a virtual space for idea exchange.

- b) The loss of traditional forms of communication.

- c) The decrease in the value of personal interactions.

- d) The uniformity of cultural expressions worldwide.

Reading Passage 3: "Exploring the Depths of the Ocean"

In the vast expanse of the world's oceans lies a realm that remains largely unexplored and mysterious. The deep sea, a place where sunlight barely reaches, is home to some of the most unusual and fascinating creatures on Earth. Scientists and explorers have long been intrigued by this underwater world, seeking to uncover its secrets. Dr. Elena Martinez, a marine biologist, is among those leading the charge in deep-sea exploration. On her latest expedition aboard the vessel Ocean Voyager, Dr. Martinez and her team descended into the abyssal depths using a submersible equipped with the latest technology.

As they ventured deeper, the team encountered a landscape unlike any other, filled with bioluminescent organisms and peculiar geological formations. One of the most significant discoveries was a new species of bioluminescent jellyfish, which Dr. Martinez named Lumina Spectra. This finding not only added to the catalog of marine species but also provided insights into the adaptability of life in extreme environments.

Dr. Martinez's exploration also shed light on the impact of human activities on these remote ecosystems. Traces of microplastics were found even at these great depths, highlighting the pervasive nature of pollution. This revelation underscored the need for more sustainable practices to protect these uncharted and fragile habitats.

Questions:

1. **Main Idea**: What is the primary focus of the passage?

   ○ a) The technological advancements in deep-sea exploration.

    ○ b) The discovery of a new species of jellyfish.

    ○ c) The exploration of the deep sea and its significance.

    ○ d) The impact of human activities on the ocean.

2. **Developmental Pattern**: How does the passage develop its ideas?

    ○ a) By outlining the history of ocean exploration.

    ○ b) Through a narrative of a specific scientific expedition.

    ○ c) By presenting a debate on environmental issues.

    ○ d) Through descriptions of various deep-sea creatures.

3. **Word Meaning in Context**: As used in the passage, "abyssal" most nearly means:

    ○ a) Dangerous.

    ○ b) Mysterious.

    ○ c) Deep and vast.

○ d) Lifeless.

4. **Character's Fear**: What concern might Dr. Martinez have regarding her discovery?

○ a) The jellyfish could be endangered by further exploration.

○ b) The discovery might not be accepted by the scientific community.

○ c) Pollution could threaten the newly discovered species.

○ d) The bioluminescent properties might not be unique.

5. **Textual Evidence**: Which part of the text best supports the answer to the previous question?

○ a) Lines discussing the discovery of Lumina Spectra.

○ b) Descriptions of the bioluminescent organisms.

○ c) Observations about the geological formations.

○ d) The mention of microplastics found in the deep sea.

6. **Character Analysis**: How does Dr. Martinez approach her deep-sea

exploration?

   ○ a) With caution and concern for the environment.

   ○ b) Focused solely on scientific discovery.

   ○ c) With excitement overshadowing potential risks.

   ○ d) Indifferent to the impact of human activities.

7. **Purpose of a Paragraph**: The main purpose of the last paragraph is to:

   ○ a) Advocate for the protection of ocean habitats.

   ○ b) Highlight the achievements of Dr. Martinez.

   ○ c) Emphasize the need for more deep-sea expeditions.

   ○ d) Criticize the lack of funding for ocean research.

8. **Word Meaning in Context**: In the context of the passage, "bioluminescent" most likely refers to:

   ○ a) Capable of withstanding extreme pressure.

◦ b) Emitting light through a biological process.

◦ c) Having a jelly-like texture.

◦ d) Being newly discovered.

9. **Character's Motivation**: Why is Dr. Martinez's discovery of Lumina Spectra significant?

◦ a) It challenges existing theories about deep-sea life.

◦ b) It offers potential for new underwater technology.

◦ c) It demonstrates the diversity of life in the deep sea.

◦ d) It may lead to new pharmaceutical developments.

10. **Textual Evidence**: Which section provides evidence for the impact of human activities on the deep sea?

◦ a) The description of the submersible's capabilities.

◦ b) The narrative of descending into the depths.

◦ c) The discovery of Lumina Spectra.

- d) The mention of microplastics in the passage.

Reading Passage 4: "The Complexities of Gift-Giving"

Every day, millions of people engage in the ritual of gift-giving for various occasions, ranging from holidays to personal celebrations like weddings, birthdays, and anniversaries. This frequent activity often evokes mixed feelings among gift-givers. Many people cherish the opportunity to give gifts as it allows them to strengthen bonds with loved ones. However, others find the task daunting, fearing their gifts might not meet the recipients' expectations.

Anthropologists view gift-giving as a beneficial social practice with significant political, religious, and psychological implications. Economists, on the other hand, are less enthusiastic. They argue that gift-giving can lead to a waste of resources, as people often buy gifts that the recipients wouldn't choose themselves or spend more than the recipients would. This discrepancy, known as the "deadweight loss of Christmas," suggests that gift-givers struggle to accurately predict what others will appreciate—a fact not surprising to social psychologists. Studies have shown that people often find it difficult to consider others' perspectives, being prone to egocentrism and attribution errors.

Despite being experienced in both giving and receiving gifts, people tend to overspend on gifts, failing to use their insights effectively. This over-expenditure might stem from the assumption that the cost of a gift directly correlates with the recipient's level of appreciation. However, this link may not be as strong as gift-givers believe. The passage suggests that gift recipients may not base their appreciation on the gift's price as much as givers assume.

Questions:

1. **Main Idea**: What is the central focus of the passage?

   - a) The economic implications of gift-giving.

   - b) The emotional experience of receiving gifts.

   - c) The complexities and implications of gift-giving.

   - d) The cultural differences in gift-giving practices.

2. **Developmental Pattern**: How is the passage primarily structured?

   - a) As a comparison of different viewpoints.

   - b) As a chronological history of gift-giving.

    ○ c) As an argument against gift-giving.

    ○ d) As a narrative of personal gift-giving experiences.

3. **Word Meaning in Context**: As used in the passage, "daunting" most nearly means:

    ○ a) Time-consuming.

    ○ b) Challenging.

    ○ c) Exciting.

    ○ d) Worthwhile.

4. **Character's Perspective**: What perspective do economists have on gift-giving?

    ○ a) They see it as a beneficial social practice.

    ○ b) They believe it leads to unnecessary waste.

    ○ c) They view it as a crucial economic activity.

    ○ d) They consider it a minor aspect of economic theory.

5. **Textual Evidence**: Which part of the text best supports the economists' viewpoint?

- a) Discussion of the "deadweight loss of Christmas."

- b) Description of the mixed feelings among gift-givers.

- c) Analysis of the psychological implications of gift-giving.

- d) Reference to studies on perspective-taking.

6. **Psychological Analysis**: According to social psychologists, what common error do gift-givers make?

- a) Misjudging the recipient's taste.

- b) Underestimating the importance of the occasion.

- c) Struggling to understand the recipient's perspective.

- d) Prioritizing the cost over the meaning of the gift.

7. **Purpose of Details**: Why do the authors mention gift-givers' experiences in both roles?

○ a) To highlight the joy of gift-giving and receiving.

○ b) To criticize the commercialization of gift-giving.

○ c) To demonstrate the challenge of applying personal insights.

○ d) To show the evolution of gift-giving practices.

8. **Interpreting Assumptions**: What assumption about gift-giving is questioned in the passage?

○ a) That recipients prefer expensive gifts.

○ b) That gift-giving is an outdated practice.

○ c) That gifts reflect the strength of a relationship.

○ d) That gift-giving should be a reciprocal process.

9. **Analyzing Motivations**: What motivates gift-givers to overspend, according to the passage?

○ a) The desire to impress the recipient.

○ b) The belief in a link between cost and appreciation.

○ c) The pressure of societal expectations.

○ d) The joy of shopping for gifts.

10. **Evaluating Implications**: What implication does the passage suggest about gift-giving?

   ○ a) It is more about the giver's intentions than the recipient's needs.

   ○ b) It often fails to achieve the desired emotional impact.

   ○ c) It can lead to financial strain for the giver.

   ○ d) It is an essential part of maintaining relationships.

Reading Passage 5: "The Art of Classical Music"

In recent times, classical music seems to have taken a backseat in the popular culture landscape, overshadowed by contemporary genres. However, its impact on the world of music and the arts is undeniable. Classical music, with its roots in Western culture, spans a period from the 11th century to the present day. This genre is not just about Beethoven, Mozart, or Bach; it encompasses a wide array of styles and compositions that have evolved over centuries.

The beauty of classical music lies in its complexity and the emotional depth it offers. It's a genre that demands attention and intellectual engagement from its listeners. Unlike much of today's popular music, which often focuses on catchy melodies and rhythms, classical compositions are characterized by their intricate harmonies and dynamic contrasts. They often tell a story or convey a range of emotions without the use of words.

Classical music also plays a significant role in education and cognitive development. Studies have shown that listening to or playing classical compositions can enhance memory, attention, and spatial-temporal skills. It's not just about producing virtuosos; engaging with this music fosters discipline, creativity, and a deeper appreciation for artistic expression.

Despite its perceived decline in mainstream popularity, classical music continues to thrive in concert halls, opera houses, and educational institutions. It remains a vital part of our cultural heritage, resonating with audiences who seek a more profound musical experience.

Questions:

1. **Main Idea**: What is the primary focus of the passage?

   ◦ a) The history of classical music.

o b) The decline of classical music in modern times.

o c) The characteristics and impact of classical music.

o d) The comparison between classical and contemporary music.

2. **Characteristics of Genre**: How is classical music described in the passage?

   o a) As a genre with catchy melodies and rhythms.

   o b) As a genre requiring intellectual engagement and offering emotional depth.

   o c) As a music style limited to a few famous composers.

   o d) As a fading art form with little relevance today.

3. **Inference**: What can be inferred about the author's view of classical music?

   o a) They believe it is outdated and no longer valuable.

   o b) They appreciate its complexity and emotional richness.

     ○ c) They find it less engaging than contemporary music.

     ○ d) They view it solely as an educational tool.

4. **Role in Education**: According to the passage, what role does classical music play in education and cognitive development?

     ○ a) It is essential for becoming a professional musician.

     ○ b) It helps in enhancing memory and spatial-temporal skills.

     ○ c) It is not as effective as contemporary genres in education.

     ○ d) It is primarily used for teaching history and culture.

5. **Textual Evidence**: Which part of the text supports the idea that classical music requires active listening?

     ○ a) The mention of its roots in Western culture.

     ○ b) The description of its complexity and emotional depth.

     ○ c) The reference to its evolution over centuries.

     ○ d) The comparison with catchy contemporary melodies.

6. **Impact on Listeners**: What impact does the passage suggest classical music has on its listeners?

   o a) It provides a simple and relaxing experience.

   o b) It fosters creativity and a deeper appreciation for art.

   o c) It primarily entertains without much intellectual involvement.

   o d) It is challenging for audiences to understand and enjoy.

7. **Author's Purpose**: Why does the author mention classical music's continued presence in concert halls and opera houses?

   o a) To illustrate its decline in popularity.

   o b) To argue for its preservation.

   o c) To show that it remains a vital part of cultural heritage.

   o d) To compare it with other forms of musical expression.

8. **Word Meaning in Context**: As used in the passage, "resonating" most nearly means:

- a) Echoing.

- b) Creating.

- c) Reflecting.

- d) Connecting emotionally.

9. **Comparing and Contrasting**: How does classical music differ from contemporary music according to the passage?

- a) It is less known and recognized by modern audiences.

- b) It focuses more on harmonies and contrasts rather than just melodies.

- c) It is not used in educational settings.

- d) It lacks the emotional depth found in contemporary music.

10. **Evaluating Themes**: What theme is prominent in the passage about classical music?

- a) Its adaptability to modern musical trends.

- b) The nostalgic value of classical music.

- c) The timeless and profound nature of classical music.

- d) The need for classical music to evolve to stay relevant.

STOP THE CLOCK

If you still have time, use it to review the questions. Don't haste. Take these final moments to ensure that you've answered each question to the best of your ability and that you haven't missed any details.

Congratulations on completing this practice session! You've taken an important step in your SAT preparation. Let's now take the time to evaluate your answers. This is a crucial part of your learning process, as it helps you understand your strengths and identify areas where you may need further improvement. Remember, every question you review is an opportunity to deepen your understanding and refine your test-taking skills. Let's begin the evaluation.

Reading 1: "The Impact of Renewable Energy"

1. c) The global effort to reduce carbon emissions through renewable energy.

2. b) The author views it as a necessary step for environmental preservation.

3. c) Nuclear

4. c) To illustrate the multifaceted nature of transitioning to renewable energy.

5. c) Changes in both infrastructure and energy consumption habits.

6. c) Is crucial for both environmental and economic reasons.

7. b) "The shift towards renewable energy is...a socio-economic one."

8. b) It offers a sustainable alternative with less environmental impact.

Reading 2: "The Evolution of Communication Technology"

1. a) The historical development of communication methods.

2. b) Carrier pigeons

3. c) It has globalized communication, making it instantaneous and widespread.

4. b) To highlight the negative aspects of communication evolution.

5. a) By emphasizing the slower pace of historical methods.

6. c) A rise in privacy violations and the spread of misinformation.

7. c) Enabled faster and more efficient ways of sharing information.

8. a) The creation of a virtual space for idea exchange.

Reading 3: "Exploring the Depths of the Ocean"

1. c) The exploration of the deep sea and its significance.

2. b) Through a narrative of a specific scientific expedition.

3. c) Deep and vast.

4. c) Pollution could threaten the newly discovered species.

5. d) The mention of microplastics found in the deep sea.

6. a) With caution and concern for the environment.

7. a) Advocate for the protection of ocean habitats.

8. b) Emitting light through a biological process.

9. c) It demonstrates the diversity of life in the deep sea.

10. d) The mention of microplastics in the passage.

Reading 4: "The Complexities of Gift-Giving"

1. c) The complexities and implications of gift-giving.

2. a) As a comparison of different viewpoints.

3. b) Challenging.

4. b) They believe it leads to unnecessary waste.

5. a) Discussion of the "deadweight loss of Christmas."

6. c) Struggling to understand the recipient's perspective.

7. c) To demonstrate the challenge of applying personal insights.

8. a) That recipients prefer expensive gifts.

9. b) The belief in a link between cost and appreciation.

10. a) It is more about the giver's intentions than the recipient's needs.

Reading 5: "The Art of Classical Music"

1. c) The characteristics and impact of classical music.

2. b) As a genre requiring intellectual engagement and offering emotional depth.

3. b) They appreciate its complexity and emotional richness.

4. b) It helps in enhancing memory and spatial-temporal skills.

5. b) The description of its complexity and emotional depth.

6. b) It fosters creativity and a deeper appreciation for art.

7. c) To show that it remains a vital part of cultural heritage.

8. d) Connecting emotionally.

9. b) It focuses more on harmonies and contrasts rather than just melodies.

10. c) The timeless and profound nature of classical music.

24

Writing and Language Test: 35 MINUTES, 40 QUESTIONS

Welcome to the Writing and Language Test section, a crucial part of your SAT preparation. This section is designed to assess your ability to revise and edit texts, ensuring they are clear, effective, and conform to the conventions of standard written English. You have 35 minutes to complete 44 questions, a task that will test both your language skills and your time management abilities.

DIRECTIONS:

In this section, you will encounter a series of passages, each accompanied by a number of questions. These questions are designed to challenge your understanding of how to effectively express ideas and how to make editorial decisions to improve the quality of writing.

As you work through this section, you will encounter two primary types of questions:

1. **Revising for Content and Clarity**: Some questions will ask you to consider how a passage might be revised to enhance the expression of ideas. This could involve rephrasing for clarity, reorganizing sentences or paragraphs for better flow, or modifying the tone to better suit the context.

2. **Editing for Grammar and Conventions**: Other questions will focus on correcting errors in sentence structure, usage, or punctuation. This will require a keen eye for grammatical rules and an understanding of standard English conventions.

Additionally, some passages or questions may include graphics, such as tables or graphs. These are provided for you to consider as you make your revising and editing decisions.

The questions will either direct you to an underlined portion of a passage or to a specific location, asking you to think about the passage as a whole. After reading each passage, choose the answer to each question that most effectively improves the passage or that aligns with the conventions of standard written English.

Many questions will include a "NO CHANGE" option. Select this option if you believe the best choice is to leave the relevant portion of the passage as it is.

Remember, this test is not just about finding errors but also about understanding the best ways to communicate ideas effectively and clearly. Your ability to analyze and refine these passages will be key to your success in this section.

Good luck, and approach each question with a critical and thoughtful mindset!

Practice Passage 1: "Revitalizing Urban Green Spaces"

Urban green spaces, like parks and community gardens, have long been an integral part of city landscapes. They provide a respite from the concrete jungle, offering residents a place to relax, exercise, and connect with nature. In recent years, there has been a growing movement to revitalize these spaces to enhance their accessibility and ecological benefits.

[1] City planners and community groups are increasingly recognizing the importance of these areas not only for their aesthetic value but also for their

role in promoting public health. [2] Well-maintained parks can offer a range of activities, from walking trails to playgrounds, which encourage physical activity and social interaction. [3] Moreover, green spaces contribute to the environmental health of urban areas by improving air quality and providing habitats for wildlife. [4] However, many urban green spaces have been neglected, resulting in underutilized and sometimes unsafe areas.

Efforts to revitalize these spaces often involve redesigning them to meet the needs of the local community. [5] This can include adding new facilities, such as sports fields or community centers, and improving safety measures. [6] Engaging the community in the design and maintenance of these spaces is crucial for their long-term success. [7] When residents are involved in the process, they are more likely to take pride in these areas and use them regularly.

Questions:

1. **Main Idea**: What is the primary focus of the passage?

   ○ a) The history of urban green spaces.

   ○ b) The importance of maintaining urban parks.

   ○ c) The revitalization of urban green spaces.

○ d) The challenges faced by city planners.

2. **Relevance of Detail**: Which choice provides the most relevant detail in the context of the passage?

○ a) NO CHANGE

○ b) from walking trails to playgrounds, thereby improving community health.

○ c) from walking trails to playgrounds, which are often overcrowded.

○ d) from walking trails to playgrounds, especially in densely populated areas.

3. **Word Choice**: As used in the passage, "Moreover" most nearly means:

○ a) Additionally.

○ b) However.

○ c) Despite this.

○ d) Similarly.

4. **Sentence Structure**: Which choice corrects an error in sentence structure?

- a) NO CHANGE

- b) However, many urban green spaces, have been neglected,

- c) However many urban green spaces have been neglected

- d) However; many urban green spaces have been neglected,

5. **Logical Sequence**: To make the paragraph most logical, sentence 4 should be placed:

- a) where it is now.

- b) after sentence 1.

- c) after sentence 2.

- d) after sentence 3.

6. **Delete or Keep**: Should the writer delete the underlined sentence in the second paragraph?

○ a) Yes, because it introduces an unrelated idea.

○ b) Yes, because it repeats information stated earlier.

○ c) No, because it provides important context for the revitalization efforts.

○ d) No, because it transitions smoothly into the next paragraph.

7. **Word Choice**: Choose the option that best maintains the tone of the passage.

○ a) NO CHANGE

○ b) as

○ c) similar to

○ d) like

8. **Consistency and Clarity**: Choose the option that ensures consistency and clarity.

○ a) NO CHANGE

- ○ b) adding

- ○ c) addition of

- ○ d) to add

9. **Transitional Logic**: Choose the transitional phrase that best connects the ideas in the passage.

- ○ a) NO CHANGE

- ○ b) Consequently,

- ○ c) In contrast,

- ○ d) For example,

10. **Concluding Idea**: What is the best concluding sentence for the passage?

- ○ a) NO CHANGE

- ○ b) As such, these revitalization projects are vital for urban development.

- ○ c) Therefore, urban green spaces should be expanded in all cities.

○ d) Hence, community engagement is key to the success of these spaces.

Practice Passage 2: "The Renaissance of Local Bookstores"

In an age dominated by digital media and online giants, local bookstores are experiencing a surprising renaissance. These cozy havens, once thought to be on the brink of extinction, are finding new ways to thrive in the modern marketplace. They are no longer just places to buy books; they have transformed into community centers, offering a variety of events and personalized services.

[1] One of the key factors behind this revival is the unique experience that local bookstores provide. [2] Unlike online retailers, these bookstores offer a sense of community and a personal touch that cannot be replicated digitally. [3] Many host author readings, book clubs, and children's story hours, creating a cultural hub in their neighborhoods. [4] Furthermore, independent bookstores often curate their selections to reflect the interests and needs of their local communities. [5] However, the rise of e-books and online shopping still poses a significant challenge to these small businesses.

To compete with digital platforms, many local bookstores have expanded their offerings. [6] This expansion often includes selling e-books and audiobooks, providing a cafe or lounge area, and even offering subscription services. [7] By diversifying their services, these bookstores can attract a wider range of customers and create additional revenue streams. [8] Community support also plays a critical role in the success of these establishments.

Questions:

1. **Main Idea**: What is the central theme of the passage?

   o a) The challenges faced by local bookstores.

   o b) The competition between digital and physical bookstores.

   o c) The resurgence of local bookstores in modern times.

   o d) The impact of e-books on traditional bookstores.

2. **Relevance of Detail**: Which choice adds the most relevant detail to sentence 2?

   o a) NO CHANGE

   o b) these bookstores offer a welcoming ambiance and personalized book recommendations.

- ○ c) these bookstores can't compete with the convenience of online shopping.

- ○ d) these bookstores are smaller and less efficient than online retailers.

3. **Word Choice**: As used in the passage, "curate" most nearly means:

- ○ a) Preserve.

- ○ b) Restrict.

- ○ c) Select.

- ○ d) Decorate.

4. **Sentence Structure**: Which choice corrects an error in sentence structure?

- ○ a) NO CHANGE

- ○ b) However, the rise of e-books and online shopping; still poses

- ○ c) However the rise of e-books and online shopping, still poses

    ◦ d) However, the rise of e-books and online shopping, still poses

5. **Logical Sequence**: To improve the paragraph's logical flow, sentence 5 should be placed:

    ◦ a) where it is now.

    ◦ b) before sentence 1.

    ◦ c) after sentence 3.

    ◦ d) after sentence 4.

6. **Delete or Keep**: Should the writer delete the underlined sentence in the third paragraph?

    ◦ a) Yes, because it introduces an unrelated idea.

    ◦ b) Yes, because it repeats information stated earlier.

    ◦ c) No, because it adds to the discussion of how bookstores are adapting.

    ◦ d) No, because it provides a transition to the next topic.

7. **Word Choice**: Choose the option that best maintains the tone of the passage.

- a) NO CHANGE

- b) as

- c) in addition to

- d) by also

8. **Consistency and Clarity**: Choose the option that ensures consistency and clarity in sentence 6.

- a) NO CHANGE

- b) expanding into new areas, like

- c) expansions include

- d) to expand, including

9. **Transitional Logic**: Choose the transitional phrase that best connects the ideas in the passage.

○ a) NO CHANGE

○ b) Moreover,

○ c) In spite of this,

○ d) Similarly,

10. **Concluding Idea**: What is the best concluding sentence for the passage?

○ a) NO CHANGE

○ b) Thus, the adaptability of local bookstores is key to their survival.

○ c) As a result, bookstores should focus solely on digital offerings.

○ d) Therefore, physical books are becoming obsolete.

Practice Passage 3: "The Growing Trend of Urban Farming"

Urban farming is becoming increasingly popular in cities around the world. This practice involves growing food in urban areas, often in small or unconventional spaces. It's a trend that not only provides fresh produce to city dwellers but also has numerous environmental benefits. Urban farms can be found on rooftops, in abandoned lots, and even along busy streets.

[1] One significant advantage of urban farming is its contribution to local food systems. [2] These farms offer fresh, locally-grown produce to urban residents, reducing the need for long-distance food transportation. [3] This, in turn, lowers carbon emissions associated with food distribution. [4] Additionally, urban farms often use sustainable practices, such as composting and water recycling, which further enhance their environmental impact. [5] Despite these benefits, urban farming faces challenges, including limited space and the need for specialized knowledge.

Community involvement is crucial to the success of urban farming initiatives. [6] Many urban farms rely on volunteers and local residents for their operation and maintenance. [7] These projects not only provide fresh food but also create a sense of community and connection to the environment. [8] Educational programs associated with these farms can teach city residents about sustainable agriculture and healthy eating.

Questions:

1. **Main Idea**: What is the primary focus of the passage?

   ◦ a) The environmental benefits of urban farming.

- b) The challenges faced by urban farmers.

- c) The increasing popularity of urban farming.

- d) The role of community in urban farming.

2. **Relevance of Detail**: Which choice provides the most relevant detail for sentence 2?

- a) NO CHANGE

- b) these farms decrease reliance on supermarkets and processed foods.

- c) these farms are usually more expensive than traditional farming.

- d) these farms utilize unused city spaces efficiently.

3. **Word Choice**: As used in the passage, "turn" most nearly means:

- a) Rotate.

- b) Change.

- c) Move.

○ d) Result.

4. **Sentence Structure**: Which choice corrects an error in sentence structure?

   ○ a) NO CHANGE

   ○ b) Additionally urban farms often use

   ○ c) Additionally, urban farms, often use

   ○ d) Additionally; urban farms often use

5. **Logical Sequence**: To make the paragraph most logical, sentence 5 should be placed:

   ○ a) where it is now.

   ○ b) before sentence 1.

   ○ c) after sentence 2.

   ○ d) after sentence 4.

6. **Delete or Keep**: Should the writer delete the underlined sentence in the

second paragraph?

- a) Yes, because it repeats information already stated.

- b) Yes, because it is not relevant to the topic of urban farming.

- c) No, because it highlights the role of the community in urban farms.

- d) No, because it introduces a new idea that is not explored elsewhere in the passage.

7. **Word Choice**: Choose the option that best maintains the tone of the passage.

- a) NO CHANGE

- b) depend on

- c) are supported by

- d) need

8. **Consistency and Clarity**: Choose the option that ensures consistency and clarity in sentence 6.

○ a) NO CHANGE

○ b) rely heavily on

○ c) are reliant on

○ d) have reliance on

9. **Transitional Logic**: Choose the transitional phrase that best connects the ideas in the passage.

○ a) NO CHANGE

○ b) Consequently,

○ c) Despite this,

○ d) Additionally,

10. **Concluding Idea**: What is the best concluding sentence for the passage?

○ a) NO CHANGE

○ b) Therefore, urban farming is revolutionizing the way cities think about food.

- c) Hence, urban farming faces an uncertain future.

- d) Thus, the key to successful urban farming is technological innovation.

Practice Passage 4: "Revolutionizing Learning Through Technology"

The integration of technology in education has revolutionized the learning experience. Schools and universities around the globe are increasingly adopting digital tools to enhance teaching and foster interactive learning environments. This shift from traditional methods to technology-based education is reshaping how students learn and how teachers instruct.

[1] One notable change is the increased accessibility of educational resources. [2] With the advent of online platforms, students can access a vast array of information and learning materials beyond their textbooks. [3] This access not only broadens their knowledge base but also encourages independent learning. [4] In addition, digital tools like educational apps and interactive software make learning more engaging and personalized. [5] However, the digital divide remains a significant challenge, as not all students have equal access to these technologies.

Embracing technology in the classroom has its advantages, but it also requires careful implementation. [6] Teachers need to be trained in using these tools effectively to enhance, not replace, traditional teaching methods. [7] Moreover, there must be a balance between screen time and interactive, hands-on learning experiences. [8] Proper integration of technology can lead to more collaborative and dynamic learning experiences.

Questions:

1. **Main Idea**: What is the primary focus of the passage?

   ○ a) The challenges of implementing technology in education.

   ○ b) The benefits of using digital tools in learning environments.

   ○ c) The transition from traditional to technology-based education.

   ○ d) The training required for teachers in digital classrooms.

2. **Relevance of Detail**: Which choice adds the most relevant detail to sentence 2?

   ○ a) NO CHANGE

   ○ b) students can easily surpass the limitations of traditional classroom learning.

- c) students often become overwhelmed by the abundance of available information.

- d) students are more reliant on technology than on teachers.

3. **Word Choice**: As used in the passage, "broadens" most nearly means:

- a) Intensifies.

- b) Expands.

- c) Complicates.

- d) Lightens.

4. **Sentence Structure**: Which choice corrects an error in sentence structure?

- a) NO CHANGE

- b) In addition digital tools like

- c) In addition, digital tools, like

    ○ d) In addition; digital tools like

5. **Logical Sequence**: To improve the paragraph's logical flow, sentence 5 should be placed:

    ○ a) where it is now.

    ○ b) before sentence 1.

    ○ c) after sentence 2.

    ○ d) after sentence 3.

6. **Delete or Keep**: Should the writer delete the underlined sentence in the second paragraph?

    ○ a) Yes, because it contradicts the main argument of the passage.

    ○ b) Yes, because it is irrelevant to the topic of technology in education.

    ○ c) No, because it highlights a crucial aspect of using technology in classrooms.

    ○ d) No, because it provides an effective transition to the next paragraph.

7. **Word Choice**: Choose the option that best maintains the tone of the passage.

- ○ a) NO CHANGE

- ○ b) should be equipped

- ○ c) must learn

- ○ d) are required to understand

8. **Consistency and Clarity**: Choose the option that ensures consistency and clarity in sentence 6.

- ○ a) NO CHANGE

- ○ b) Teachers need training

- ○ c) Teachers, needing training

- ○ d) It is necessary for teachers to be trained

9. **Transitional Logic**: Choose the transitional phrase that best connects

the ideas in the passage.

- ○ a) NO CHANGE

- ○ b) Despite this,

- ○ c) Additionally,

- ○ d) As a result,

10. **Concluding Idea**: What is the best concluding sentence for the passage?

- ○ a) NO CHANGE

- ○ b) Thus, technology is transforming education for the better.

- ○ c) Therefore, the future of education lies solely in digital advancements.

- ○ d) Consequently, traditional teaching methods are becoming obsolete.

STOP THE CLOCK.

Good job! Let's now review the correct answers for all four passages:

Passage 1: "The Impact of Renewable Energy"

1. c) The exploration of the deep sea and its significance.

2. b) Through a narrative of a specific scientific expedition.

3. c) Deep and vast.

4. c) Pollution could threaten the newly discovered species.

5. d) The mention of microplastics found in the deep sea.

6. a) With caution and concern for the environment.

7. a) Advocate for the protection of ocean habitats.

8. b) Emitting light through a biological process.

9. c) It demonstrates the diversity of life in the deep sea.

10. d) The mention of microplastics in the passage.

Passage 2: "The Evolution of Communication Technology"

1. a) The historical development of communication methods.

2. b) these bookstores offer a welcoming ambiance and personalized book recommendations.

3. a) Additionally.

4. a) NO CHANGE

5. a) where it is now.

6. c) No, because it adds to the discussion of how bookstores are adapting.

7. b) as

8. a) NO CHANGE

9. b) Consequently,

10. b) Thus, the adaptability of local bookstores is key to their survival.

Passage 3: "Exploring the Depths of the Ocean"

1. c) The resurgence of local bookstores in modern times.

2. b) these farms decrease reliance on supermarkets and processed foods.

3. c) Select.

4. a) NO CHANGE

5. c) after sentence 2.

6. c) No, because it highlights the role of the community in urban farms.

7. c) in addition to

8. b) expanding into new areas, like

9. a) NO CHANGE

10. b) Therefore, urban farming is revolutionizing the way cities think about food.

Passage 4: "Revolutionizing Learning Through Technology"

1. c) The transition from traditional to technology-based education.

2. b) students can easily surpass the limitations of traditional classroom learning.

3. b) Expands.

4. c) In addition, digital tools, like

5. d) after sentence 3.

6. c) No, because it highlights a crucial aspect of using technology in classrooms.

7. b) should be equipped

8. b) Teachers need training

9. c) Additionally,

10. b) Thus, technology is transforming education for the better.

Reviewing these answers will help you understand your strengths and areas where you might need further practice. Keep up the good work, and continue refining your skills for the SAT Writing and Language Test!

25

Math Test

Welcome to the Math section of our practice test. In this section, you will have the opportunity to tackle 30 questions that cover a range of mathematical topics:

- **Algebra**: You'll encounter questions that focus on solving equations, simplifying expressions, and working with variables.

- **Geometry**: This section will test your knowledge of areas and perimeters of different shapes, properties of circles, and various geometric concepts.

- **Probability**: You will be introduced to basic probability calculations, including scenarios involving marbles and other probabilistic situations.

- **Statistics**: This part of the test involves calculations related to averages, medians, and modes.

Unlike the real SAT, there is no time limit for our practice test. You will receive immediate feedback after answering each set of 10 questions. However, it's essential to keep in mind that the actual SAT includes approximately 44 questions, and you will have 70 minutes to complete them. The real test may also feature more questions involving graphs and data interpretation.

Another important distinction is that the official SAT is administered in a digital format. This means you will have access to an online calculator during the test, which can be a valuable tool for solving more complex problems.

Now, let's get started with the Math section of our practice test. Remember that the goal is to familiarize yourself with various types of mathematical problems and build your problem-solving skills. Good luck!

No.	Question	Option A	Option B	Option C	Option D
1	What is the value of x in 5x + 7 = 32?	4	5	6	7
2	Area of a rectangle with a length of 15 cm and a width of 8 cm.	120 cm²	130 cm²	140 cm²	150 cm²
3	Probability of drawing a red marble from a bag with 2 red, 5 blue, and 3 green marbles.	1/4	1/3	2/5	2/10
4	If 4z - 6 = 10, what is z?	3	4	5	6
5	The median of five numbers is 10. If four of the numbers are 8, 11, 9, and 12, what is the fifth number?	10	9	11	12
6	Perimeter of a square with a side length of 9 cm.	36 cm	27 cm	18 cm	45 cm
7	Solution to 5t - 3 = 17.	2	4	6	8
8	If the radius of a circle is 6 cm, what is its diameter?	12 cm	18 cm	24 cm	30 cm
9	Simplify the expression: 3(2y + 5) - 4y.	2y + 15	10y + 15	6y + 15	6y + 5
10	The sum of the interior angles of a quadrilateral is:	360 degrees	270 degrees	180 degrees	90 degrees

Let's check the first 10 answers

No.	Correct Answer
1	c (6)
2	a (120 cm²)
3	c (2/5)
4	d (6)
5	c (11)
6	a (36 cm)
7	b (4)
8	a (12 cm)
9	c (6y + 15)
10	c (180 degrees)

These answers correspond to questions that cover algebra, geometry, and probability, providing a comprehensive practice experience for the SAT Math section.

Here are the next 10 questions for you:

No.	Question	Option A	Option B	Option C	Option D
1	What is the value of x in the equation 2x + 6 = 20?	6	7	8	9
2	What is the area of a square with a side length of 7 cm?	49 cm²	50 cm²	57 cm²	70 cm²
3	If a bag contains 5 yellow, 3 blue, and 2 red marbles, what is the probability of drawing a yellow marble?	1/2	5/10	5/8	5/11
4	Solve for y in the equation 7y - 4 = 17.	3	5	4	6
5	The average of four numbers is 25. If three of the numbers are 20, 30, and 25, what is the fourth number?	20	30	40	50
6	What is the perimeter of an equilateral triangle with a side length of 8 cm?	24 cm	25 cm	26 cm	32 cm
7	Find the solution to the equation 4m + 5 = 21.	3	4	5	6
8	The circumference of a circle is 62.8 cm. What is the radius? (Use π ≈ 3.14)	10 cm	20 cm	15 cm	30 cm
9	Simplify the expression: 4(3a + 2) - 5a.	7a + 8	12a + 8	17a + 8	12a - 2
10	What is the sum of the interior angles of a pentagon?	5⁀0 degrees	360 degrees	450 degrees	720 degrees

Good job!
Let's check how well you did:

No.	Correct Answer
1	c (8)
2	a (49 cm²)
3	c (5/8)
4	c (4)
5	c (40)
6	a (24 cm)
7	b (4)
8	a (10 cm)
9	b (12a + 8)
10	a (540 degrees)

Here are the last 10 questions for you:

No.	Question	Option A	Option B	Option C	Option D
1	What is the value of x in the equation 3x - 9 = 15?	8	6	5	7
2	What is the area of a circle with a radius of 6 cm? (Use π ≈ 3.14)	113.04 cm²	120 cm²	132 cm²	144 cm²
3	If a bag contains 6 orange, 4 green, and 5 blue marbles, what is the probability of drawing an orange marble?	3/5	6/15	6/10	6/11
4	Solve for p in the equation 8p + 5 = 37.	4	5	6	7
5	The mode of five numbers is 12. If four of the numbers are 12, 15, 12, and 18, what is the fifth number?	12	15	18	20
6	What is the perimeter of a regular hexagon with a side length of 5 cm?	30 cm	35 cm	40 cm	45 cm
7	Find the solution to the equation 6n - 7 = 29.	4	6	5	7
8	A rectangle has an area of 48 cm² and a width of 6 cm. What is its length?	8 cm	7 cm	9 cm	10 cm
9	Simplify the expression: 5(2x - 3) + 7x.	17x - 15	10x - 15	17x + 15	10x + 15
10	What is the sum of the interior angles of a hexagon?	720 degrees	540 degrees	360 degrees	900 degrees

Amazing!
Let's check how well you did this time:

No.	Correct Answer
1	a (8)
2	a (113.04 cm²)
3	d (6/11)
4	c (6)
5	a (12)
6	a (30 cm)
7	b (6)
8	a (8 cm)
9	a (17x - 15)
10	a (720 degrees)

In this practice chapter, we covered 30 questions, providing a comprehensive overview of key areas you'll encounter in the SAT Math section. These questions spanned various mathematical topics, including:

- **Algebra**: Focusing on solving equations, simplifying expressions, and working with variables.

- **Geometry**: Covering areas and perimeters of different shapes, properties of circles, and other geometric concepts.

- **Probability**: Introducing basic probability calculations with marbles and other scenarios.

- **Statistics**: Involving calculations of averages, medians, and modes.

On the actual SAT, you can expect approximately 44 questions and will be allotted 70 minutes to complete them. The real test will likely include more graphs and data interpretation questions, and it's important to note that the format will be digital. This means you will have access to an online calculator during the test, which can be a valuable tool for solving more complex problems.

As you have seen in these 30 questions, it's crucial to have a strong grasp of fundamental mathematical concepts and problem-solving skills. The SAT Math section is designed not only to test your mathematical knowledge but also to assess your ability to apply this knowledge in different contexts.

Remember, during the actual test, if you finish before the allotted time, it's wise to use the remaining time to reevaluate your answers. Double-check your calculations and ensure that you have read each question carefully. This practice can help you catch and correct any errors, potentially improving your overall score.

Preparing for the SAT Math section involves regular practice and familiarization with various types of mathematical problems. By working through practice questions like these, you're on the right path to developing the skills and confidence needed for success on the SAT. Keep practicing, and good luck!

26

The Final Words

In this book we've set out on a journey to demystify the SAT, an essential milestone in your pursuit of higher education. Together, we've explored the structure, format, and content of this standardized test, equipping you with the knowledge and strategies needed to approach it with confidence.

Throughout this guide, you've gained valuable insights into each section of the SAT, from the Reading and Writing section to the Math section. We've provided detailed information about various question types, offered practice questions and answers, and shared tips and techniques to enhance your performance.

Here's what you've learned:

1. **In-Depth Understanding:** You now possess a thorough comprehension of the SAT's format, including the number of questions, timing, and question types in each section.

2. **Effective Strategies:** You've acquired valuable strategies for approach-

ing different question types, managing your time, and maximizing your score.

3. **Practice Opportunities:** You've had the chance to practice with numerous SAT-style questions, allowing you to apply what you've learned and refine your skills.

4. **Digital SAT Insights:** We've covered the transition to the digital SAT, ensuring you're prepared for the test's digital format and online calculator.

5. **Time Management:** You recognize the importance of efficient time management during the test, as well as the advantage of guessing when uncertain.

6. **Upcoming Test Dates:** You're informed about the anticipated SAT test dates and registration deadlines for 2024, giving you the flexibility to plan your test-taking strategy.

As you prepare to take the SAT, keep in mind that success is not solely about mastering the material but also maintaining a positive mindset. Embrace challenges as opportunities for growth, and view each practice question as a chance to improve.

You possess the skills needed to excel on the SAT. Believe in your abilities, stay focused, and remain dedicated to your goals. With persistence and the knowledge you've gained from this guide, you are well on your way to achieving the scores you desire.

Remember that the SAT is just one step in your academic journey. It doesn't define your worth or limit your potential. Your dedication, hard work, and determination will open doors to a brighter future.

So, go ahead, approach the SAT with confidence, and take that important step toward your dreams. You've got this! Best of luck on your SAT journey, and may your future be filled with success and opportunities.

Made in the USA
Monee, IL
26 March 2024

55878881R00090